Little Bible
Thumper

A story of
restoration and redemption

Freida M. Shingleton

PRESS

Interested in having Freida come speak to your church, conference or group? Please use the following contact information:

www.littlebiblethumper.com

Email – littlebiblethumper@gmail.com

www.xulonpress.com

I have known Freida Shingleton from the time she first came from Eire to the US. Hers is an amazing story of how God is able to redeem and save a life that was totally lost in darkness. Her story gives hope to others in similar situations who have lost their way and cannot seem to find their way out. Jesus Christ is that Way; Freida's story is a story of what Jesus can do, about His saving power. It is a story of triumph over the power of darkness and finally coming to the Light of God.

Today Freida's life is totally transformed. She is a beautiful and radiant Christian wife and mother. She has a life and has a wonderful story to tell. I recommend this book to everyone!

Rev. Christopher Alam
Dynamis World Ministries

Watching Freida Shingleton become the beautiful woman, wife and mother she is today has been an absolute joy. Her life and testimony will show anyone and everyone that divine appointments can happen to you even when you are on the other side of the world. This book is honest, heartfelt and a moving account of an amazing journey, full of heart and wisdom.

Rev. Julie Beemer
CLUB1040 Director and Author of the children's series
"Around the World with Matt and Lizzy"

Freida Shingleton has allowed us into her life by highlighting that no matter how far you are from God, His pursuit never stops. With vulnerable moments from her own experiences, this book will inspire you to never settle for an ordinary life. As you read through this exciting story you will be motivated to seek God's best for yourself and share it with others. This is a must read!

Rev. Norm Dubois
Lead Pastor
East Coast Believer's Church
Oviedo, FL

I would like to introduce you to the ministry of Freida Shingleton. I have had the pleasure of knowing Freida closely for over a decade because she is my daughter-in-law. If I had to choose one word to describe her that word would be: Genuine. Freida is very open and honest; therefore everything you read in this book can be taken at face value. Much like the Bible, Freida portrays in this book both the frailty of sinful man and the goodness of a loving God.

If you feel that you have made too many mistakes in life to ever be happy again or you've let God down too many times to receive forgiveness, please read Freida's story and you'll understand that there's no such thing as "beyond redemption" when you turn to God with your whole heart.

I highly recommend this book!

Rev. Guinn Shingleton
Former Lead Pastor
Faith Outreach Family Church
Terre Haute, IN

Having the greatest privilege to minister to many many people throughout the years, we continually are on the lookout for good resources that can truly make a difference in the lives of those we are so blessed to help! This book is a treasure, filled with precious and powerful riches, confirming Gods inexhaustible pursuit of His children.

As you turn each page, the invitation to join Freida on her journey will be irresistible! Real, sometimes raw, yet so beautiful, powerful and life changing! Freida we love you...

Pastors Paul and Karen Brady
Pastors and Overseers,
Living Rivers Trust (NI)
Millennial, Tulsa OK, USA.

Awesome grace beyond imagination! A riveting and unvarnished story of God's relentless pursuit!

Pastors Ron and Sandy Johnson
Senior Pastors and Overseers
One Church
Longwood, FL

"Little Bible Thumper" is an amazing testimony of how God can take a person out of darkness and into the light, from the deepest pit of addiction to solid ground, from the continent of Europe to a new life in the U.S. When we were recently introduced to Freida M. Shingleton, it was like meeting true family. Her love for Jesus and her heart for people is the real thing, and you can almost feel her heartbeat as you turn the pages in this book. It is genuine, honest and covered by grace. The Scriptures and the "Key Points Review" in each chapter is a great tool, even for reading groups that will make you meditate and pray as you read on. With this book Freida takes you on a journey. It is her genuine hope that her story will help people out of bondage and transform lives, which we firmly believe that it will!

Pastors Christian and Karen Hedegaard
Senior Pastors and Founders
Powerhouse Church
Orlando, FL

Dedication

I dedicate this book first and foremost to Jesus Christ. Through His enduring love I am rescued from the grip of darkness and delivered into a life of peace, joy, contentment, and amazing love.

Also, to my handsome husband who persevered with me through some horrendous trials along the way. You never gave up on us and have helped teach me how to walk with Jesus. You've helped to keep my feet, and your own, on the path of life when they faltered.

Tessa, my beautiful daughter, I dedicate this book to you. You are a child of joy and light for Jesus in this dark world!

To my father and late mother, whom I love very, very much. You both worked hard all of your lives and provided and loved the best you knew how. I look forward to being with you, and our entire family, for all eternity in Heaven!

I love each of you with all of my heart!

Table of Contents

ACKNOWLEDGMENTS

T hank you, Jesus, for giving me the inspiration to write this book in an effort to help women avoid falling into the devil's snares. It's a story about Him, and a story about you, as much as it is about me.

Thank you, amazing husband Chris, and beloved daughter Tessa, for loving me, despite my imperfections, or maybe because of them!

Appreciation to Northlands Addiction Treatment Centre in Northern Ireland. You are amazing, doing a great work saving lives and families. I can't say how much you've meant to me.

I want to acknowledge Pastors Paul and Karen Brady for being a part of my delivery out of darkness.

Thank you to Pastors Matt and Julie Beemer, who have also played a significant part in my journey.

To our great friend, Rev. Christopher Alam, who has inspired me over the past many years and showed me Jesus' heart, and the kind of Christian that I want to be.

To Pastor Norm and Dina for helping teach me the Word of God.

To my parents-in-law, Guinn and Karen, for always loving and supporting me.

Thank you to my talented, loving step-children – Victoria, Judah, Luke, and Annalise – you are a real blessing to my life and I love you!

Finally, but certainly not least, thank you to my friend Amanda Hamilton, who first took my pencil and paper scribblings and typed all diligently.

Introduction

He Stood with Me

*Now for a brief time GOD, our God, has allowed us, this battered band, to get a firm foothold in his holy place so that our God may brighten our eyes and lighten our burdens as we serve out this hard sentence. We were slaves; **yet even as slaves, our God didn't abandon us.***

(Ezra 9:8-9 MSG emphasis added)

I woke up rattled, perspiring and eyes wide open, but my mind was blank as I tried to make sense of the urgency of the dream! Why would I be dreaming of her? Why on earth would I be dreaming of an urgent need to go see my Mum?

Perhaps it was my conscience and I was feeling the same old guilt for my dismissive behavior towards her the last time we were together. That had been my usual treatment of her over the last few years. She frustrated me with her victim mindset, unremitting self-pity, her lack of forgiveness towards Dad, and seething bitterness. I had my own problems, but she didn't seem to care about those.

The urgency hit again, only this time it felt even more persistent, determined to get my attention. I needed to go see her, today! I knew I was hearing God and sensed this visit was for my good, not hers.

It was a five and one-half hour trip one way and meant a day off work, but this was one directive I could not disobey or hide from. God was clearly telling me I must tell her I love her and that I was sorry.

Two days later, celebrating my thirtieth birthday in Amsterdam, I realized why God had me clear my conscience and make peace with her. I got the phone call that she was dead.

Years of alcohol abuse had numbed my emotions so they could no longer flow naturally from me. I didn't know how to react to the news. Over the years, I had felt eruptions of burning hot anger, fear, guilt, and despair spew over me violently at times when I thought of her, but right then no feeling was there. It was like I could choose the emotions I would use to deal with my mother's death in the same objective way I might choose a book to read. I would be cool and accepting as I downed beer after beer and added a few joints of hashish. That would drive the real, unfelt grief deep down into my soul.

All the years of stuffing pain down into my dark soul had worked well for a season, but pain like that cannot remain undealt with. It would not remain unfelt forever. It wouldn't allow me to forget it. Eventually, it would choose its time to make itself known. The greatest challenge of my life lay ahead of me, when all that pain would come rushing to the surface to try to suffocate and destroy me.

A war for my soul took on a new ferocity; the safety net now seemed missing. The battle for my freedom from bondages, born out of lies that had strongholds on me, commenced in earnest! My human strength was pitted against our age-old enemy, a battle I was doomed to lose, but forced to fight to survive.

Jesus had made His appearance and introduced Himself to me at the age of four. Though I was not aware of it, He never left me. When I needed Him the most, He stood with me during my devastating encounters and battles with evil. He was there with me in my darkest hours. My eventual victory was secured because He had already paid my ransom and set me free.

My story is how I came out of the devil's bondages to claim as my own the freedom Jesus had already bought for me.

Chapter 1

The Child I Was

The grass was sun-bleached and flattened in circles around me where I lay. I breathed in the sweet scent of sun-ripened hay and the dusty old donkey laying a few feet from me.

Merryweather was the unwilling recipient of my childish love; a love that endured through kicks, bites, trampling, and foul glares. If I approached slowly and without too much obvious stealth, I was able to soothe her suspicious nature and get close enough to stroke the soft white fur of her nose, run my hand gently over her sun-frazzled coat, and enjoy the tickle of her tiny thinning black mane.

The black cross on her back reminded me what a holy beast she was, picked out and favored by our father despite her character flaws. I loved her so! I loved her beautiful dark brown eyes that were half covered by those long eyelashes that allowed her to doze yet remain consciously aware of my encroaching presence.

Our home was grand and sprawling while the Irish countryside crept up close to its feet and stretched out like a textured, color-soaked tapestry to the faraway white fences. It was an old property, once a stone quarry that still carried the deep scars of the mining that left us with ponds and luxurious vegetation. It was a wonderful playground for my boundless imagination and home to my best friends, Merryweather the donkey, my beloved pony

Viva, two badly behaved goats, and a small squadron of self-important ducks.

To my young mind, Dad was surely the King of the Universe, a powerful handsome Warrior Lord, a Legend among men, yet remote and somewhat untouchable for me. This added to my awe and reverence of him. I could admire him from afar and feel pride swell my heart and glorify in his presence when bestowed with the delight of his company.

My three older sisters were all just like him. They were bigger than me, his replicas in female form, magnificent and strong in my young adoring eyes. I felt so proud to be born into this family, even though I knew I didn't really fit. I lacked a lot of the qualities they had; the hardness of heart, the ruthlessness. I was a soft-hearted animal lover, and a dreamer who was no match for their sharp words and piercing comments.

As the family black sheep, I dreamed of becoming as tough as I saw them to be. Mum was of different stock, too. By her own admission, she and I were misfits, viewed as an inferior batch. My Mum reinforced these beliefs in me. When stressed and struggling with her own emotions, she would lash out at me with condemning words.

She struggled to have control over her daughters and often lost her temper due to the lack of respect she received. When she lost her temper, she wounded all of us from time to time with callous, angry words. She once called me ugly and compared my looks and behavior very negatively against her friend's children. These comments really hurt, and though I lodged them away deep inside my mind, they surfaced later to feed an inferiority complex during those critical teenage years.

Though I saw Mum as a damaged person and a product of a loveless childhood, I started to harbor anger and bitterness toward her for those hurtful words. The knowledge that I was looked down upon by those I loved hurt me a lot, but the damage that was done by this unacceptance bit at my soul much more deeply than I was aware of growing up. Satan was planting his seeds of anger and insecurity in my heart to use against me in the future.

"Those who hurt us are usually hurting themselves,
and their pain may be so strong that they are not even aware
they are hurting us." – Joyce Meyer

Most of my time was gloriously taken up with one adventure after another with our dogs and pets. I so reveled in the outdoors and romping with my animal family that the twisted thread of deceit and hateful competition that grew within the walls of our home was barely visible to me at first.

However, in the shadows, Satan was relentlessly spinning his webs of captivity around my soul. Those chains were called anger, insecurity, bitterness, and hate. I only came to see these strongholds in me when I grew older and tried to remove their very negative effects out of my life. Each stronghold which held me captive was formed out of a lie, which needed to be rooted out. Later in life, those lies would hold me prisoner in a living hell.

Freida, the Little Bible Thumper

This family joke started when the lady pulling a little wagon with "Jesus" painted on the sides idled up our driveway. This kind lady asked my Mum if she had any children who would like to attend Sunday School.

I had spied the lady from behind my Mum and was drawn to her warmth and genuine kindness. I asked if I was to go with her, and Mum was glad to pass me off to someone else. We drove to a small, white plastered stone church standing alone on top of a hill, a few miles from my home. It was winter and my clothes were not really adequate against the chill in the air that day. Snow still covered the ground and the heating in the church did not work.

However, the warmth that flowed from that Christian lady as she sat with me was exquisite. Having never experienced such acceptance and caring, I never wanted to leave her. She kindly led me through the Salvation Prayer, and I knew in my heart that something huge had happened to me that day. I was only four years old, and I didn't comprehend the magnitude of the decision I had made nor the benefits that came with it, but the seeds were planted deep in my heart. My solo church attendance fell away and with it my memory of having dedicated my life to Jesus, but His light and joy never left me.

Throughout even some of my worst times,
the joy of the Lord has been a strength to me!

Undercurrents of Darkness

Life in the house became more and more turbulent. Mum and my sisters just didn't get along well and there was always some sort of disagreement going on between them. I felt nervous much of the time at home, endeavoring always to fly underneath everyone's radar and stay out of trouble. All the backbiting between my sisters and between them and Mum was very distressing. It seemed like there was a constant state of contention and conflict.

The only source of comfort inside the house for me were the family dogs that I adored. In fact, we were inseparable and went everywhere together. There was safety with the dogs and they loved unconditionally. They never judged me or had mood swings or behaved unpredictably, so they were my perfect companions. I was deeply comforted by them and I learned how to receive and give love due to them.

Growing up, I began to overhear a lot of malicious attacks on the character and looks of others. I once watched intrigued as some of my family members actually fashioned voodoo dolls to resemble people in their lives they did not like. They would impale these dolls with pins and speak curses over their intended victims.

Months later, I heard them nervously chattering how one of these people whom they had cursed in this way had become ill. People were very concerned as they had discovered the lady had some form of cancer scare. There was mostly a dark atmosphere in our home.

At one point, things became so unsettled they even forgot my ninth birthday. Hurt and confused, I collected lots of drugs from the medicine cupboard and dissolved them in a mug of water. Then in a fit of anger, I attempted to drink this vile mixture to teach Mum a lesson for not giving me the attention and love I so craved and for not protecting me from the daily open contempt I received from my siblings.

The concoction was revolting, and as I regained my senses, I realized the senselessness of my suicidal adventure. Instead, I decided to leave the vile, harmful concoction sitting on top of my bedroom drawers for Mum to find. I hoped this discovery would highlight for her the depth of my inner turmoil. However, she never did make that discovery, and I finally discarded that unused overdose, which was just further evidence that no one cared for me.

I felt very isolated and alone, with no one to love me but the animals. During the summer break, I decided to ask my neighbor, Willie-Sam, who often drove me to horse events, if he could take me and my pony to my Aunt Jennifer's, ninety miles away. He agreed to drive us both there, so I left with my pony, the clothes on my back, no money, and without telling another soul where I was going. As it turned out, I was away on this adventure for a full three weeks before anyone noticed I was gone! A search commenced to locate me, but it was more out of amused curiosity than care, it appeared.

God Was Still There

> *Though my father and mother forsake me,*
> *the LORD will receive me.*
> (Psalm 27:10 NIV).

Still, I saw God in everything outside of the house during those childhood years. The beauty of the soft sycamore leaves fluttering in the breeze sent tiny flashing messages of joy and love to my heart in shades of yellow and green. God shone in the soft hazy beams of light that came through the tree canopies to light spots of the undergrowth where I occasionally caught sight of a rabbit or a hedgehog foraging. The sounds of nature were a rhapsody to my ears, a holy worship of God, the Creator Himself. It was outside in nature that I found the peace only God could give me.

Then there was my Aunt Bonnie, my Dad's sister. She was a flamboyant, gregarious, fun, eccentric character who lived by the sea in a beautiful coastal village on the North Coast of Ireland. Bonnie would have me stay the occasional weekend with her in her cozy home with its dramatic views of the stormy sea and its ever changing character.

She always lit her home with small lamps that flooded the home with a soft yellow warmth that often contrasted the furious blue-gray seas that would crash the craggy coastline and spray the stone house with salty sea mist.

On balmy summer evenings when the sea would be calm and a beautiful shade of golden green, Bonnie would take me out upon it in her little wooden boat to fish for mackerel. We could see the deep sandy bottom shining back at us in the sinking sun's light.

The little flashing silver fish beneath us darted, and bit excitedly, at our bait and we soon filled a basket of them. It was my greatest pleasure to sink into the still green waters and swim about the wooden boat as Bonnie would regale me with charming stories of her youth in her soft, charismatic laughing voice. We would later fry those mackerel in butter and lemon juice. They were the tastiest fish I ever remember having.

I loved my Aunt Bonnie and I cherish those memories with her. Although she showed no signs of believing in God, she knew how to live in a way that showed Him to me. His warmth, love, and provision for us were apparent through the peace her home exuded. The majestic beauty He created for us to live in and enjoy thrilled me and awakened the artistic nature within me.

Some thirty years later, I had the opportunity to witness God's love to my Aunt Bonnie before she left this earth. I pray she received Jesus into her heart so that we will meet again in joy and love, somewhere even more beautiful and vivid than here.

I loved God and His creation. If life could have consisted solely of those warm and peaceful times, this book would have been very different. However, storm clouds were on the horizon, rushing toward us at a very high speed. They were coming to end my idyllic childhood and thrust me into a life of not knowing who or what to cling to. If only I knew then what I know now. If I had only known God is the only rock, the only safe place, and the only hope for any of us, things might have gone totally differently.

I learned that God can be trusted to love us unconditionally and hold us in His hand through a life full of turbulence and disappointments.

Abandoned

It started with my father coming home late one evening, looking haggard and extremely distraught. My mum ushered me off to bed and I went without quibbling with ears finely tuned for I knew something serious was afoot, and I was afraid.

My father's distress was due to a very heated argument he'd just had with his business partner, his older brother Tom. My dad and Uncle Tom had been in business together since their teenage years. They had worked hard and between them generated a lot of wealth. However, money had begun to go missing in large chunks and the brothers blamed one another. A war was waged between them that completely split our families.

We later discovered a family member who had worked as my father's personal assistant had been the one syphoning the unaccounted for money and covering her tracks. At the time, though, my Uncle Tom blamed my father. He was so hurt by the seeming betrayal, he threatened my father saying he was going to bomb our home and disclose my father's secret liaisons with another woman to my mum!

The last threat was the only one that actually bore fruit, and the results were catastrophic. My mother's heart was broken and proved to be unrepairable without her reliance upon Jesus to help her. The brothers were alienated until just before Tom's death, thirty years later.

For me, the fallout of this traumatic time was huge. The devastation of my parents' marriage began to affect my mother's ability to be my caretaker.

After an evening of socializing, and perhaps drinking more than she ought to, my mum woke me up very late one evening weeping inconsolably at the end of my bed and warned me over and over to never trust anyone, no matter how much I thought that they loved me!

I was angry with her and with dad. I felt they were moving our family farther and farther from my dream of being a happy, secure family where we all loved and looked out for each other.

I made a vow at that exact time to never let any of them or anyone else close to my heart again, especially men.

If this is what a man had reduced my mum too, then I swore the same would never happen to me.

The minute I made that vow I shut out God's voice in my life. I went on to live my life in accordance with that foolish vow, and not God's guidance and leading. My heart also hardened towards others, and Him.

Later in life I had to ask God to forgive me for making that vow, and to help me soften my heart in order to receive His love, and to be able to love and trust Him and others.

In an attempt to start over, my parents purchased a scenic second home (it was an old salmon fishery on the coast) and left to live there, leaving me virtually alone in the country home at seven years old. Mum basically quit the task of being a mother to me, leaving the chore to my sisters, who were now leaving the home as quickly as they could by any means possible.

For them, this chore was intolerable and they made that clear to me. In truth I felt I had been abandoned by the family that was supposed to love and care for me. A kind neighbor drove me back and forth to school and became my sole friend.

Mum made a visit to the old home once a month to see that the freezer had enough frozen goods and to ensure our dogs had a supply of food. I never saw any of that food. I was too young to cook and had no idea how to de-frost and make the freezer food edible. My sisters took care of themselves. I often resorted to eating the dog's biscuits and emptying boxes of dry food. I basically relied on whatever food I received at school, and even took to stealing food from other kids. I comforted myself with the thought that mean kids deserved it!

I lived in an isolated, lonely, loveless existence until the age of fourteen. I may have felt abandoned through this time, but at least my home was familiar and I felt stable there. However, even bigger changes were coming.

The Move

Dad decided we needed to sell my childhood home, the one constant I had in my life. He and Mum now were living permanently in the salmon fishery. They were invested completely in the catching of wild salmon and making a great livelihood selling the huge wild salmon to hotels and restaurants around the country.

To continue my schooling, I was required to live with a family member, her husband, and their three young children. Dad paid a handsome fee to them for my board. The house was small; I shared a bedroom with one of the young children. I no longer had my personal space or any of the pets or countryside adventures that brought me joy. I was unwanted by all in my new abode and again living in an environment of conflict and strife. They made it clear I was a burden.

During this phase of life, I felt my parents had really let me down. They seemed consumed only with their own lives, their own desires, and I had been thrown to the side, unwanted, discarded, someone else's burden!

Life became even harder as I left my tiny school and moved to another with a harsher environment, where bullies thrived. The new school was a terrifying place for me, where I felt certain I would be eaten up by all the confident, self-assured, aggressive teenagers I was thrown amongst.

These other youth unconsciously recognized a wounded peer, and much like life in the animal kingdom, they saw me as easy prey. Being the brunt of cruel jokes and enduring the disrespect of one's peers are devastating blows for the heart of one already feeling insecure and trying to find her identity.

I had never been interested in dating and now suddenly boys were the topic of discussion of every girl around me. I felt very awkward around boys. I was not as mature as the girls around me and still interested in childish things. I was woefully unprepared for this scene, with my short boyish haircut and my small collection of out-of-date clothes which were ill-fitting, unfashionable, and rarely washed. I felt like a fish out of water, flailing for breath, washed up on the beach. Boys noticed me, but if any paid me attention, my painfully awkward personality caused them to shy away from me and I was a source of amusement for many. The result was I felt like a joke, in a constant state of humiliation at school and at my new "home."

Around this time, one of my sisters who had jumped into an unwise marriage in her pursuit of love and security, started to experience difficulties with her husband and his numerous infidelities began to come to light. She and my dad approached me and asked if I had ever witnessed him acting "odd" around me. The truth is I had, but did not feel safe in sharing anything with them. My insecurity had already begun to breed seeds of distrust so I kept my thoughts to myself. They persisted as if they already knew the truth, so eventually I shared I had received very inappropriate vibes coming from him when alone in his company.

This information travelled straight back to him, and of course, he completely denied any strange behavior towards me. Word went out around my family that I had made up lies and fantasies about this person for attention and to cause my sister further upset. I had no way to convince them I had not been lying. I deeply regretted ever trusting my family and felt extremely betrayed once again.

The result was that anger was continually being sown into my heart. There was anger at my family whom I had believed and trusted, but had failed to protect me. Everyone in my life seemed cruel, self-promoting, and heartless. The God of my childhood seemed less real, less accessible, and less powerful than this life of harsh realities unfolding before my eyes.

My anger was partly turned toward God for I felt He should have stepped in and made Himself my protector. Little did I know He was with me and never ever left me. He cried when I cried and laughed when I laughed and kept me through it all.

"For I know the plans I have for you," declares the Lord, "plans to prosper you and not to harm you, plans to give you hope and a future. Then you will call upon me and come and pray to me and I will

listen to you. You will seek me and find me when
you seek me with all your heart. I will be found by
you," declares the Lord, "and will bring you back
from captivity." (Jeremiah 29:11-14a NIV)

A Journey of Restoration and Redemption

As you read of my journey of restoration and redemption, I pray you will meet the Restorer and receive healing for your broken heart just as I did. As I take you along on my journey, I want to encourage you to begin to implement the truths I have learned so you too can break the chains that have kept you bound in a life of pain, addiction, abuse, betrayal, or neglect.

We will stop at the end of each chapter and review some key points or lessons you might benefit from in your own journey. Then I will challenge you to ask yourself some questions designed to get you started on your own journey to restoration and redemption.

Key Points Review

➤ I came out of the devil's bondages to claim as my own the freedom Jesus had already bought for me.

➤ "Those who hurt us are usually hurting themselves, and their pain may be so strong that they are not even aware they are hurting us." – Joyce Meyer

➤ Throughout even some of my worst times, the joy of the Lord has been a strength to me!

➤ *Though my father and mother forsake me, the LORD will receive me.* (Psalm 27:10 NIV)

➤ I learned that God can be trusted to love us unconditionally and hold us in His hand through a life full of turbulence and disappointments.

Ask Yourself…

Have I ever said to myself, if only I knew then what I know now?
What was I going through at that time in my life?
Did I know God at that time in my life?
What have I learned as I have gone through my own turbulence and disappointments?

Read Jeremiah 29:11-14a and use these verses to write a prayer thanking God that He has always had His hand on your life and has been watching over you even during your turbulent times.

Chapter 2

Child in Chains

To feed us a damaging lie about ourselves, the devil may use someone who is an acquaintance, a beloved friend, a relative, or images we see on TV and magazines to speak and imprint the lie in our minds.

Such lies can be a simple throw-away comment or a more hurtful invalidation. Either way, the lie sinks down into our souls and negatively affects the way we view ourselves. The bondage comes next, when we accept a harmful way of living to help us cope with the lie that has been eating us alive from the inside out.

Many lies were deposited in my soul in my growing years, and to counteract them and feel like I was worthy to receive love, I embraced many forms of bondage, not seeing them for what they really were.

I see so clearly now that every instance of bondage
that we allow to imprison us starts with a lie.

The devil is a long-term strategist and his greatest pleasure is to warp us into compliance with his weapons of destruction. He wants us all to be in bondage ourselves and also devises ways to make such lifestyles look good to others.

When we lose the ability to influence others into joining us in our sin and life far from God, it is at that time that the devil will try to take our lives and claim us as his own in Hell for eternity.

"For though we live in the world, we do not wage war as the world does. The weapons we fight with are not the weapons of the world. On the contrary, they have divine power to demolish strongholds. We demolish arguments and every pretension that sets itself up against the knowledge of God, and we take captive every thought to make it obedient to Christ." (1 Corinthians 10:3-5 NIV)

Alcohol

As a young teenager, it was clear that my self-esteem was deeply affected in a negative way, and when I was introduced to alcohol, the devil proved that he had laid the groundwork for my demise flawlessly.

Alcohol, from the first sip, changed my world! Through it I saw both myself and also my world so differently. Suddenly I believed that I was in fact very pretty, instead of merely stupid and awkward. I began to see myself as smart, fun, and witty.

I began to realize while intoxicated that I had in fact been gifted with many talents; I began to believe that I was athletic, likeable, and even attractive!

It was as though a dark cloud had been lifted from before my eyes, and also that alcohol was helping me see myself and the world as it really was. *The truth!* I thought to myself. Suddenly I was aware that I was all the things that my sisters were—that I was at least their equal. In beginning to believe that I was worthy of love and adoration, the sense of relief and elation was ecstasy to me, and I mused that this surely must be what Heaven feels like.

The devil had planted and watered his lies as seeds in the soil of my heart from childhood; lies that I was not good enough. He deceived me into thinking that anger and depression were a normal part of life. He whispered into my ears that ruthlessness, deceit, and betrayal were traits of the strong, the survivors of this world.

The alcohol that I poured on these seeds of lies caused me to bear much destructive fruit in my life. This negative fruit almost damaged me beyond repair and also hurt all those around me, both then and for twenty years to come!

Alcoholism became a snare of bondage in my life from the first drink, and yet for a season I truly believed that it was the greatest thing that had ever happened to me.

The Bible tells us that sin seems good for a season, but that it will turn on you in time. (See Hebrews 11:25, which speaks of the "fleeting pleasures of sin", and Numbers 32:23, which says, "You may be sure that your sin will find you out.")

This was very true in regards to my experience with a sinful lifestyle. I found out that the devil will not turn your sin, such as an addiction, against you, until he has you fully hooked and at his absolute mercy–of which he has none!

Once the devil has you physically dependent on a substance, he will drag you through humiliation after humiliation in your pursuit of your drug, and he will cause you to derail your life and hurt those you love and those who love you.

Once I had uncorked the bottle, it was a very deep bottle indeed...with no bottom in sight!

With care and caution thrown to the wind, I embraced
the devil's invitation to play in his backyard.

I decided to forsake all that was decent, moral, and of good character; and because of my choices, I commenced a horrible downward spiral into darkness.

Eating Disorder

At age eighteen, I started a three-year season of training to become a Registered General Nurse. Unfortunately, alcohol was still working its magic on me personally, and then since I was living away from home and earning my own money, drinking became a much more serious pursuit.

My mind became saturated with all sorts of unsavory things that the world deems beautiful, and I did not feel that I measured up to the images I was blasted with every day. As a result, I began to diet, which progressed into starving myself and eventually into the full-blown eating disorders of anorexia and bulimia.

Eating disorders are a horrible, deadly, and obsessive type of addiction, a type of bondage from which it is very difficult to be set free. My experience with eating disorders threatened to steal my health, youthful looks, sanity, and life. Of course, this was the fruit born directly from the lie that I had ingested, regarding how I was not good enough just as I was.

Dieting and throwing up to decrease and control my weight became virtually all I thought about every day for the next ten years. At times, my desire to eat would nearly drive me crazy, and if I succumbed to my temptations to eat normally, I would not stop at normal amounts but instead I would overeat grossly. Afterward, as a cyclical pattern, I would feel consumed with guilt and self-hatred, and would then have to purge and throw it all back up again.

The stomach acid from my constant vomiting was rotting my teeth and was causing me to develop extremely painful esophageal ulcers. And yet my heavy drinking ran along unabated, and most weekends were a dirge of dark, humiliating memories.

The devil operates through the world's media, shoving images constantly at young women of how they "should look." These images often display unhealthily thin women, and the images are enhanced surgically and digitally to achieve a look that is very unrealistic for the average girl. A percentage of the world's population does have the ectomorph body type whereby they are naturally slender and tall, but it is dangerous to hold up one body type as superior over all others.

What chance do young women have for growing up to healthy maturity in the midst of the spiritual and emotional sickness of this world, perpetuated by those who do not know Jesus and His never-ending, unconditional love for us just as He made us?

Foundation of God's Word

This world, where Satan seeks to usurp God's authority, feeds us with unrealistic expectations on how we should look, act, think, and live. These are all lies meant for our dissatisfaction with ourselves and consequently for our harm. But God's Word speaks just the opposite to us, telling us the truth of how He created us.

> *For you created my inmost being; you knit me together*
> *in my mother's womb. I praise you because*
> *I am fearfully and wonderfully made."*
> (Psalm 139:13&14a NIV)

Without the Word of God saturating our minds, we fall into believing Satan's lies about us and our lives. The world and the people who make the unreachable standards for us are only tools of the devil, driven by their worldly lusts for wealth, notoriety, and status.

They decide that a certain image is the pinnacle of beauty, and we—like lambs to the slaughter—follow and spend much of our lives futilely trying to transform our bodies, our minds, our children, and our homes into the images we are bombarded with in magazines, TV, and the cinema.

We often spend huge amounts of money that we don't have, using large resources of our energy and time, while we make the world and its unhealthy culture richer and ourselves increasingly more miserable and disillusioned.

Yes, we should take of care of ourselves, but from a heart where God is 1st place and the very center of our existence. Otherwise our sadness and lack of fulfillment makes us easy prey to all the worldly pursuits that promise happiness, peace, joy, and satisfaction. These positive aspects of life come from one true source alone; they will never come from this world's system and what it has to offer, which only delivers eventual pain, disappointment, despair, ruin, and destruction.

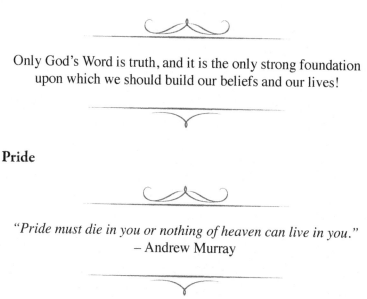

Only God's Word is truth, and it is the only strong foundation upon which we should build our beliefs and our lives!

Pride

"Pride must die in you or nothing of heaven can live in you."
– Andrew Murray

A lie sown into my mind from an early age was that I was born into a family of people who were in every way superior to others. I got the wrong impression that my family was smarter, more athletic, more capable, invincible, stronger, and better looking than everyone else. And although I felt that I didn't measure up to this superior standard, I believed I would one day.

Pride found fertile ground in me and grew ridiculously huge, helped along by alcohol and the delusions of grandeur that came with alcoholism. Pride also came by being focused on myself. My self-consciousness became self-centeredness, and I took my focus completely off God and placed it onto myself instead.

I became my own god. I didn't follow God or even care what He had to say about any decisions I would make, because I became the judge of my own actions. I deemed anything that I wanted to do, that brought temporary pleasure, as fit and good.

If anyone found fault with me, it would threaten my growing pride. I would then bolster myself with more prideful delusions about who I was, and I would completely rebel against anyone who tried to offer kind guidance.

As a result, what started off as self-consciousness and fear of what others thought of me evolved into arrogance, haughtiness, and extreme egotism. Excessive pride in oneself is one of the devil's ploys to divide us from God. It makes humility impossible and something to be scorned. Without humility we cannot please God, for we cannot take our eyes off ourselves and place them firmly and solely on Him.

Pride does not allow us to drop to our knees and repent before our Living God for our sins. It does not allow us to ask Him to come into our lives and wash away the sin and the lies within us, so that we may live pure and clean, free from bondage.

Instead, pride drives us down the road of destruction and prevents us from turning around. It makes us become hard and calloused as it propels us through one painful event after another.

Those that take the hedonistic route, as I did, will eventually be broken by the pain that they are bringing upon themselves by living outside of God's will and protection, and they will fall on their faces and cry out for our God to help them! This is when God can come in and start a restoration in our hearts and minds.

I learned that without repentance, there can be no change, and without a change of direction, there can be no restoration.

Looking for Escape

I wanted to flaunt my new hard-won, slim physique, and nightclubs and pubs were the ideal place to do that. The alcohol gave me the fake confidence and security to be around other people and to enjoy their company and admiration.

I often would wake up the next morning in cold, dirty student quarters with a strange guy. I did not have blackouts, so fortunately I was always able to recall the previous night's events, and these misadventures were never of a sexual nature. I was always a great disappointment in that regard for my suitors, because I was not looking for sex. I wanted and needed love, security, and comfort, and I was looking for these things to be freely given to me. I had no intentions of giving anything in return, only receiving.

Similarly, I had odd characters wake up with me in my tiny nurse's home room, which was always awkward; and these people never did give me the security, love, or comfort that I so needed.

It was a very lonely, soulless time in my life, during which I really believed that everyone was disposable and worth very little, as I apparently was.

Anger at my parents grew within me as I blamed them for my lonely status in life. I thought that the emptiness in me was because they had abandoned me and had failed to love me the way that I saw that my friends were loved and cherished by their families.

But the hole in me was a God-sized hole, and I didn't come to realize that until my mid-thirties, so I had ten more years ahead of me to seek that love and sense of belonging in all the wrong places.

In my anger with my Mum and Dad, I stayed away from them for longer and longer stretches of time, and I became increasingly desperate to meet someone with whom I could escape my tortured existence.

"Be alert and of sober mind. Your enemy the devil prowls around like a roaring lion looking for someone to devour. Resist him, standing firm in the faith, because you know that the family of believers throughout the world is undergoing the same kind of sufferings." (1 Peter 5:8&9 NIV)

Key Points Review

➢ The devil had planted and watered his lies as seeds in the soil of my heart from childhood – lies that I needed to recognize in order to come into God's freedom for my life.

➢ The Bible tells us that sin seems good for a season, but that it will turn on you in time.

➢ *You knit me together in my mother's womb.* (Psalm 139:13 NIV)

➢ Only God's Word is truth, and it is the only strong foundation upon which we should build our beliefs and our lives.

➢ I learned that without repentance, there can be no change, and without a change of direction, there can be no restoration.

Ask Yourself...

What lies, either about myself or others, have I allowed the devil to plant in my life?
What is one powerful example of personal repentance that I have experienced?
Which area of bondage described by the author can I most relate to?
What is one truth in God's Word that I need to remind myself of in my present circumstances?

"Do not conform to the pattern of this world, but be transformed by the renewing of your mind. Then you will be able to test and approve what God's will is—his good, pleasing and perfect will." (Romans 12:2 NIV)

Read Psalm 139:1-18 and choose one verse from this passage to write in a visible place in your home, until you can repeat the verse from memory.

Chapter 3

Marriage and Career Unraveled

I met my husband-to-be when I was eighteen. Oscar was a local boy from Portrush. He was the oldest of seven children and came from staunch Catholic stock. His was a loving, warm, fun family. I met Oscar while visiting his family with my parents. He was the first good thing to happen to me in my teenage years. He was kind, responsible, and good-looking, and he wanted to make a good life for us by working his way up in the business world; but most exciting of all to me was that he wanted to live outside of Ireland. He had set his sights on Northern England, and I loved the thought of leaving my troubled youth behind me.

Oscar's parents, brothers, and sisters were very welcoming, and their home was warm and always seemed celebratory. I fell in love with the whole family. I took them into my heart as my own family and I tried to replace the hurts inside me with their kindness and stability.

Oscar and I began a relationship which quickly led to an engagement, and we were both so elated and excited about our future together. What I believed to be real love bloomed promisingly during those days. He began an apprenticeship for an accounting firm in Northern England, and I stayed behind in

Northern Ireland to complete my nurse's training in Belfast. We were able to see each other every several months when we could afford to travel to one another, but being apart was extremely difficult for me and I was very lonely.

During this time of being apart, my eyes began to wander because I so sought companionship and acceptance. Before long I met another young man from England, and alongside my relationship with Oscar I commenced a similar relationship with this person. With them both living in England, it was easy for me to keep the two relationships separate and unknown to one another.

I knew that my duplicity was wrong and that I was mistreating both of these young men, whom I believed I loved and who in return believed they loved me! This situation went on for the full three years of my nurse's training.

A Huge Decision

When I qualified as a Registered General Nurse, I had a huge decision to make: I would need to move to live with one of these men and start a life together, and cut off my relationship with the other.

It was a tough time, and although my heart was already pretty calloused and hardened, I was emotionally torn between the two. Yet alongside these feelings of sadness, my arrogance was also flattered that I actually had such a choice to make, and so in my casting down of one person, along with the pain I felt a powerful high and a twisted satisfaction and pleasure in betraying and hurting one of them.

In the end I chose Oscar, because in my mind he was the better contender. Oscar was going places in the world and I wanted to go with him.

Writing a book of my life testimony now is difficult. It brings back to my memory all the things that I have done, and all the different ways I mistreated and betrayed people in pursuit of my own happiness. As a sick outcome of seeking my own agenda, hurting others never brought the hoped for, happy conclusion that I expected.

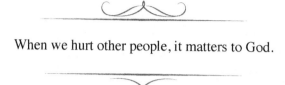

When we hurt other people, it matters to God.

God is not pleased with us when we live recklessly, carving a path through others when they stand in our way and using them for our own gain. He has put it in our hearts to feel sorrow when we cause pain to others. No matter how hard we try to stuff this pain deep down inside us, it will resurface one way or another, and repentance will be required in order to reach a place of fulfillment in our lives.

I am struggling to be fully honest as I write this book, because it is difficult to reveal the depths of depravity that I sank to over the course of my life. I treated others inhumanely and really thought little of it. When my conscience would try to prick me with guilt and regret, I would push it down and suppress it, and I would concentrate instead on drowning such uncomfortable feelings with alcohol and lustful, willful living.

A God-Sized Hole

During that time of my life, I would focus on the things that the world held dear and put all my efforts and thoughts into pursuing and achieving those things—such as wealth, glamor, and social position.

Despite my growing problem with alcoholism, I climbed the social ladder progressively; but the higher I got, the feelings of emptiness and futility became even greater inside of me. My life and all the things that I had prioritized seemed so plastic, temporal, and at times evil to me. On the other hand, the things in life that I had trampled over held great joy and comfort to others around me, such as their relationships with family members, friends, spouses, employers, and co-workers.

I came to notice that these people had a peace and calmness about them that I completely lacked and deeply craved; they didn't seem to be plagued with recurring regret, guilt, or shame. The more I spoke with these individuals, I realized that they had a completely different set of life priorities. Their lives did not revolve around themselves like mine did.

These people believed in God like I also did, but they were living differently than I was. They were living in ways that I knew were pleasing to God, and I was very interested in what they were doing to achieve the serenity and joy that they exuded.

Oscar and I commenced our marriage with an alcohol-soaked wedding full of hilarious drunken episodes by Oscar's father of singing and falling over. It was a joyous occasion, and I believed I had finally left my troubled emotional life behind me. But in reality it had not left me; instead, it was going to continue to weigh down my life and drag me deeper and deeper into darkness, and finally into complete brokenness.

We kicked off our marriage with high hopes and dreams, as two lost souls who had found one another and who desired so much to make a success of our lives. We didn't know what success meant to God. Instead, we were pursuing the world's idea of success, the one that we knew and revered. Our dreams were of wealth, prestige, materialism, travel, and partying. We really believed that these were the components of happy, successful lives.

I worked as a nurse in a plastic surgery unit (mainly reconstructive for those impacted by major accidents, etc.), which was a tough environment for me at that time of my life. Being there only helped to ferment the idea in my heart that the world was a tough, hard, unforgiving place, and that to succeed in it I had to be tougher, more resilient, and more ruthless than those around me.

Oscar's rise to wealth was very fast, and before long we were living mortgage-free in luxurious homes; I was driving a new, latest model Lotus Elise sports car; and we were living on the same street as world-renowned celebrities.

Everything that I wore was black, my car was black, my horse was black, and my dog was black. I was consumed with my image and how others perceived me. I was a celebrity in my own mind and I lived for the feelings of superiority over others around me. I had no thought of God and no need for Him. I was riding high in the world and tasting all it had to offer, living that dream in full. However, living this way never completely fulfilled or satisfied me.

There was a hole in the center of me that only God could fill.

None of these worldly things (or even Oscar) could fill my place of need inside. I dared not look too deeply into myself for answers, lest I saw the real blackness of my heart.

Unraveling

So, ever searching to feel complete and to feel satisfied, I began to move from job to job, finally settling as a manager of a nursing home. I was poorly equipped for such a position, because I was devoid of compassion for the elderly and saw them as useless and as a waste of space.

There was no care in me for others; my own needs were the only things that mattered to me, and I had a growing anger towards life itself. I was realizing more and more that my life was missing something that I was unable to find. I brought my frustration to work and treated everyone there dismissively, arrogantly, and without care.

I started to experience negative effects more frequently with alcohol. I seemed to be embarrassing myself more often–slurring words, falling over, and saying inappropriate things to people. The concerning thing was how I began to experience crushing feelings of shame and guilt the following morning, which were a new and worrisome addition to my party lifestyle.

Oscar did not know how to help me, because he did not even realize that I was dealing with alcoholism. He himself came from a drinking background and did not see my increasingly huge problem for what it was.

Missing more and more days of work due to physical and emotional turmoil was an ongoing part of my condition, adding to my shame and sense of helplessness in life. I started to look for someone to save me; after six years of marriage I was ready to jump ship.

We moved back to Ireland in an attempt to give me more stability, but this only heightened the instability, and before long I was meeting fellow alcoholics. Eventually, in this environment of hopelessness, I commenced an affair.

This incident was a fruitless, barren, short-lived romance that had nothing to do with genuine love or care for one another. After it had ended, I was totally and utterly unprepared for the absolute emotional crisis into which I then plunged headlong.

I cannot adequately describe to you the pain, the guilt, the unremitting shame and the utter despair that bombarded my mind. I thought at one point that I would lose my mind, and I would have welcomed a total emotional breakdown so that I could get help!

I needed help so badly, but I didn't know where
or from whom I could find it.

End of the Marriage

As my life and our marriage deteriorated, I tried counselors, friends, and family, but nothing worked. I was trapped in a vortex of life-threatening pain. All my wrongdoings towered in my mind all at once, and all the pain that I had stuffed down into my soul was making its visible debut in my life–and it was all so huge that it was terrifying.

However, I was not ready to give up the things in my life that were still giving me even fleeting moments of ecstasy. The partying, drinking, smoking, self-adoration, wealth-seeking, and lusting after inappropriate dangerous people had a powerful stranglehold on me.

During these terrifying lows, the fear, guilt, and shame that I experienced were becoming heart-stopping and I thought I would lose my sanity and go crazy. I would shake violently and try to hide in bed under the covers. Once again, I would seek companionship and counseling, but absolutely nothing in the world could calm my terror and my devastated nervous system.

The fear sometimes was so intense that I would tear my own hair out and wail and scream for peace, but no one would come. I had visions of ugly, obscene-looking demons crowding around me with intense, delirious glee on their hideous faces; so delighted they were with my absolute, hysterical terror!

I dreamed of dying and being set free from this prison of terror-filled nightmares. That wasn't a possibility for me, though, because somewhere along the way I had developed the belief that if I took my own life I would surely go to Hell. I didn't see how I was going to be able to live a normal life, and in fact, I did not even know how to opt out of the abnormal life I was living. The result was that I was fully stuck and quickly reaching the end of my rope.

Alcohol at this point seemed like the only reprieve from my growing depression. No matter how short-lived the tiny bit of peace was that I got from drinking, it seemed worth it just to escape the darkness. The darkness that I sunk into directly afterwards each time was ever worsening in intensity.

And yet, my pride and rebellion against
God kept me going back and continually seeking from
alcohol what only He could give me.

My marriage fell apart, ending in a divorce, and I pursued much less desirable partners who liked to drink and party like I did. For a few years in my early thirties, life was very grim and shameful for me. My conduct became increasingly erratic and I lost the respect of many people who lived around me, the people I worked with, and my friends and family.

Key Points Review

➤ When we hurt other people, it matters to God.

➤ Living in sin never completely fulfilled or satisfied me, because there was a hole in the center of me that only God could fill.

➤ I needed help so badly, but I didn't know where or from whom I could find it.

➤ My pride and rebellion against God kept me going back and continually seeking from alcohol what only He could give me.

Ask Yourself...

Is there any problem in my life that is too big for God to handle? (See Jeremiah 32:17.)
What was the lowest place I have ever been in personally? What did I learn from it?
Are there any parts of my life that I am tempted to use to fill God's place in my heart?
Who are the people that I trust the most that I can go to when I need prayer?

Read Psalm 121:1-8. Schedule a time with a friend to share honestly with each other, and to ask for God's help in areas of your lives where each of you especially need Him right now.

Chapter 4

I Knew It Was God!

In the midst of this dark season of my life, a girl at my work gave me a book one day regarding suicide and how it hurts so many outside of yourself. I believe God spoke to her heart regarding me, because I was increasingly desperate and desiring relief from life.

That book talked about Jesus and how He had come to set us free, and to cause us to live in health and joy with unbroken peace. I needed peace so very, very badly and I was at a point in my life when I was actually ready to start listening to God.

The divorce devastated my heart, and although I had not treated my husband with respect or evident love, I had loved him deeply, and now I missed him terribly. I missed the security he gave me, as well as the laughter, hopes, and dreams we had shared. All those dreams were dashed and ruined now, and the sadness that came with that reality was unbearable. I was so alone–with no support, no comfort, and no hope.

A Beam of Light

At this time, when my will to live was at its lowest, I woke up one morning and saw sunlight peeking in from outside the window. My first response was to smile, but the smile didn't get fully formed, as my mind was instantly bombarded with the horror of my reality. I lay there numb, like the living dead.

This was when I had my first supernatural experience. A beam of sunlight poured into the room and moved over to where I lay, and when it touched my outstretched hand, I felt its tangible heat. My eyes were drawn to my hand, and as I watched, a golden sparkling ball of light formed in my cupped hand! I could see for an instant what looked like a sparkling golden Christmas tree ornament. As I stared, mesmerized by this phenomenon, the golden object dissolved but soaked into the flesh of my hand. Instantly, I could feel the sensation of an effervescent tingling that began to travel up my arm, bringing with it an amazing feeling of joy, hope, and love! It reached my body and travelled all the way up to my head and down to my toes. It was electrifying!

The sensation lasted only for minutes, but it seemed like an eternity. When the experience finally dwindled away, I sat bolt upright in bed and for a full forty minutes marveled at what had taken place. I knew it was God!

The memory of that absolute joy, hope, and love has never left me, even in all the years since that time.

This experience was literally like a bright beam of light that shone into the dark, black cavern of my life; but as it diminished and faded out, the darkness came crowding back in again, leaving only a dull memory of the joy, hope, and love that I had experienced.

> *"Come now, let us settle the matter, says the Lord.*
> *Though your sins are like scarlet they shall be*
> *white as snow; though they are red as crimson,*
> *they shall be like wool."*
> (Isaiah 1:18 NIV)

Crying Out in the Darkness

I now knew that the things that I sought existed somewhere, but I still did not know how to access them. Following my unusual experience, I entered into several years of groping in the dark for comfort. I was blessed to stumble over a counselor who correctly diagnosed my alcoholism, and although I fought against that truth, a seed was planted in my life to confirm this truth.

During this period, all that had previously mattered to me was lost. I struggled to make enough money from part-time work, due to my very fragile emotional condition. Money was tight, my glamourous lifestyle gone, my beautiful home a distant memory, one of my beautiful dogs gone to a different owner, and my safety and peace a thing of the past.

I fell into one addictive, abusive relationship after another, until my heart was so torn and I was so broken that I found myself living in an awful hovel. One day I fell to the floor and cried out to God to help me. "Help me break the cycle of growing destruction!" I cried out. "Help me break free from the chains that bound me to a life of poverty, shame, and abuse!"

In that very moment, God heard me. I was broken by sin and stared death in the face, and God was the last and only hope for me.

My heart turned that day; it turned from relentlessly
and futilely seeking my own safe ground in the darkness,
and looked instead toward His light for the answers.

Afterwards, God put a godly lady in my path who invited me
to a wonderful non-denominational Christian church, where I
began to learn about Jesus and what He had done for me. It was a
mind-blowing revelation for me, and I recalled the beam of light
that I had seen in my bedroom. The surging feeling of love, hope,
and joy came back to me, stronger than ever before. The church
people embraced me and I felt I had finally found a home!

Road to Freedom

Though my life was now headed in the right direction, I was
not miraculously healed of my addiction to alcohol, and I had to
take the necessary steps to recover.

Alcoholics Anonymous is a wonderful organization that helps
many people worldwide to get back on their feet and to remain
sober throughout their lives. The people I met through the organization helped me to realize that I really did have a legitimate,
life-threatening addiction–one that couldn't be ignored but
needed to be dealt with on a daily basis.

Although it was not necessarily Christ-centered, God was a
big part of this process of recovery, and surrendering my will to
Him was vital. However, the devil was not done with his attempts
to destroy me. This time he came to me in the form of a strong,
gentle, handsome, and tall man who was a fellow recovering
alcoholic.

Sam was his name. He was kind and cheerful, with a big laugh
and a flashing white smile. He was interested in me and seemed very

concerned for my well-being. When I discovered more about him, I learned that he lived in a beautiful rural house with horses, and that he was a successful entrepreneur and a self-made wealthy man.

This relationship seemed like it was from God. However, the more time we spent together, I began to detect some character flaws in him which caused me to feel warnings in my spirit. But because the man looked so good for me in so many areas, I shoved away the inner warnings that I felt about him, as I was so practiced in doing.

The warnings that I was hearing in my heart were that he had deeply repressed reservoirs of anger inside, that he had not fully renounced alcohol in his heart, and that he had other dark secrets. However, I was willing to overlook these things and just focus on the positive side, and I decided to try with this man to rebuild my old dream of a happy family.

Sam was instrumental in getting me admitted to a rehabilitation center, which was a life-changing experience. There I learned all about the nature of alcoholism and how to live without it. I am forever thankful to the counselors and people that I met there. I shall never forget their wise words and loving kindness, which sustained me through more tough times that yet lay ahead.

Family Split

Around this time, my dad and three other family members fell into a heavy disagreement with one another over the selling of a large, substantial property that we all jointly owned.

Inadvertently I was drawn into the battle, which was led by two family members who were fueled by their old competition with the rest of us. They wanted a larger slice of the pie each, more than their fair share of the proceeds, or at least more than the rest of us were to receive from the sale.

I owned half of this particular property because my dad planned for it to be my inheritance from him, and the other half was divided between him and the other three family members.

This made me suddenly a hot commodity within my family. Through the disagreement, the family split in two. I was like a coveted bone sitting between two mad dogs. Whichever side could control me and my half of the share could control the outcome of the sale of the property—and consequently their percentage of the profits.

Both sides were very determined to achieve their desired outcome, and a very bitter battle ensued. At one point, my family member endeavored to have me committed to an insane asylum when I had a relapse with alcohol due to the strain of this extremely distressing time. Her plan was to take power of attorney over my share in the property. But I resisted the idea of being committed to a mental institution, and she could find no one willing to sign a form to forcibly commit me. In her rage, she physically attacked me, punched me to the ground, and kicked me around her kitchen floor with all her formidable, competitive weight-lifter strength!

I was wounded physically, but that was nothing compared to the emotional damage I received from this incident. My world as I knew it was now completely shattered, and there was no one to trust. I felt that everyone who I thought had loved me did not love me after all. All that I had thought was good seemed that it actually was not!

There was no solid ground for me to stand on and no strong foundation upon which to build.

I threw myself into the arms of Sam, because he was the only person who seemed to care about my well-being and my interests. Later, I came to realize that there is only One whom we can trust fully to love us unconditionally forever.

The attacking family member and I made a sort of peace with one another, although I was leery of her in the process and have remained so to this day. Shortly after that incident, she recommended that I make out a will and make her the sole beneficiary, claiming she was truly the one with my best interests at heart—despite her recent conduct towards me! Apparently she did not think that I had a good chance of living a long life, due to the way

I was living. Fortunately, God intervened and kept me and my financial interests safe; He used my father to occasionally speak up with words of wisdom..

These family members had all received their inheritances from our generous and giving father, and now two of them were trying to steal mine. On top of it all, the one who physically attacked me was someone I had adored and trusted all my life. In my mind, she had been like a mother to me, and now I was shocked to my core by the truth of how she really cared about me–not as much as I thought!

This family member never has gained control of that property or of me. She did, however, destroy her relationship with my father and alienated herself from the other family members involved. This included even the one who was her accomplice, as that one later came to her senses and quit her pursuit of greed.

I am happy to say that today I am at peace with
all members of my family, and each of them has
received Jesus as their Lord and Savior!

With the Lord's help I have forgiven each of them for their attempts to manipulate me and steal from me, for lying, and for spewing hate and vitriol about one another and to one another over the course of several years.

However, for my protection and sanity, the Lord removed me from living in proximity to them, and today I enjoy a pleasant, peaceful distance between them and me.

Growing Battle at Home

I was very vulnerable for Sam, the predator, to encroach into my life and become valuable and indispensable to me. Over time, he became more and more controlling, and he showed his anger more often over small things that I did that offended him.

I did everything I could to make him happy and to have him never find fault with me, but that was an impossibility. He became especially angry and irritable during weekends and holidays, when he remembered how he used to enjoy partying and getting wild with alcohol and women. I became his "whipping boy" when he could not handle his frustration at not being able to indulge his addiction, and he vented his anger on me.

This caused him to become extremely caustic with his words; very verbally and emotionally abusive. He threatened to break off the relationship probably fifty times in the two years we were together.

Although I no longer lived an addict's lifestyle and I was able to work as a nurse, even regaining self-respect and respect from my co-workers, I still was not happy. I battled with depression, because I never knew how this emotionally unstable man was going to behave. I had no hope for a happy future with him, and yet I was so fearful and too weak emotionally to leave him. I was fearful that I would never find anything better, so scared to be alone, and terrified of how I would survive financially without his help.

I had also become emotionally dependent on this increasingly abusive person. He was often away for evenings and overnight stays, and I knew instinctively that his explanations regarding his whereabouts were fabricated. But I constantly made excuses for him and hid the truth about him from others and from myself.

I knew that he secretly scanned my mobile phone regularly, and he asked me questions regarding who I talked to in hopes of catching me in a lie. When I said I was going somewhere, he would call the location where I had told him I would be, to check if I was really there or if I was lying. His paranoia seemed to only worsen with time, even though he never caught me in a lie. It was painful to live with him, but the prospect of living without him was terrifying!

Again I found that I was caught in a trap, and although caring friends around me were telling me to get out of the relationship (and I knew that was the advice I would give myself), I needed the decision to be made for me.

As we were approaching Christmas during our second year together, he was being disproportionately bad-tempered, even for him. He was insufferable to be around, and I noticed an internal shift within me. I found a strength within me that was finally standing up for myself, saying that enough is enough!

Because he was always extremely sensitive to everything that I did, he began to detect my heart's disengagement towards him, and it made him highly suspicious and even more watchful of me.

He had been mentioning for some time about the real estate that I owned that I ought to have some sort of will in place, in case anything should happen to me. He said that he really needed me to display my love and commitment to him by making him my sole beneficiary. He would check with me every so often to ask if I had done this, and whenever I would tell him I hadn't gotten around to it yet, he would fly into a stony rage and cut off all forms of affection towards me. He would commence a cold war against me that would last for days, as my punishment. And it really was cruel punishment, because he was all that I had as a form of security, and when he would withdraw from me I was filled with fear and insecurity.

I foolishly would appease him by telling him that I would go to my solicitor and sort it out when I could find time for an appointment, even though I had no intention of doing so at all.

Even as these circumstances continued, I had long ago planned a pleasant, romantic overnight getaway over the Christmas holidays for us together, and I decided to go ahead with the plans since it was all organized.

I know now that God had been preparing my heart for what was about to happen. He had been giving me an inner strength and untangling the attachments of my heart from this unhealthy, sick man.

Key Points Review

➤ The memory of God's beam of light, joy, and hope in my life has never left me, even in all the years since that time.

➤ My heart turned from relentlessly and futilely seeking my own safe ground in the darkness, and looked instead toward God's light for the answers.

➤ In that very moment, God heard me.

➤ Because of what God did, today I am at peace with all members of my family, and each of them has received Jesus as their Lord and Savior!

➤ Even through difficulties in my relationship, God had been preparing my heart for what was about to happen.

Ask Yourself...

What was my experience like when I first cried out to God to save me? Do I believe He is able to save me even now?
Am I seeking to grow relationships with the people in my church?
How do I handle it when family members intentionally do things to hurt me?
Do I expect God to work in my circumstances? Are there areas where I am tempted to give up?

Read Isaiah 55:6-7. Take a moment and thank God that at the very moment you cry out to Him, He is ready to hear your voice.

Chapter 5

Out of My Egypt

astle Leslie is one of the most beautiful castles in all of Ireland, set in the midst of rolling green hills, tiny stone-walled fields, and whitewashed cottages. The castle was restored to its original grandeur and exuded a wealth of history and old world majestic beauty.

The exterior had the typical castle-like appearance of old quarried stone and high turrets with tiny windows spiraling upwards to their pointed peaks. Inside there was a coolness of air that comes from being surrounded with stone floors and walls. The only hint of warmth came from huge ancient rugs thrown across the stone floors. Huge walk-in fireplaces with logs piled high waited to be lit with the setting of the sun.

This was the venue where I had booked our romantic retreat.

As we walked into the castle, I was in awe and wonder looking at the suits of armor, the occupants of which adorned the walls in ornate brass frames, staring sternly down at us. Looking back, I realize that I also felt a shiver of evil breathe coolly over my skin, but because I was so acquainted with evil, it barely registered in my conscious awareness.

We were shown to a luxurious room on the top floor inside one of the turrets, and we were amazed with the views across the multi-textured cloth of Ireland, as far as we could see.

Sam proposed a walk of the grounds before our evening dinner in the castle. On our ramble we passed by a quaint inn which looked warm and inviting, with golden light flowing from the small leaded windows and live Irish music coming from within. The music was accompanied by stomping feet and great guffaws of laughter roaring out the open front door.

I wanted to keep on walking, even though my old addictive nature yearned to stop and look in the door; so I pushed forward. Sam faltered, hesitated, and slowed his pace, pulling on my arm. I turned to look at him, knowing with fear my answer before he asked the question.

"Do you want to stop?" he asked. "I will take care of you," he said, "but I will only let you do this if you swear to follow my lead."

I only replied with a nod, acquiescing, knowing I was about to break two years of sobriety and not wanting to put words to the decision that could be held against me later.

Strangely, without explanation, Sam walked me around the entirety of the building, looking at the layout of the windows and the location of the exit doors. I knew he was checking out how to exit the building quickly if the need arose, and I should have been wise enough to walk away, but my alcoholic old self had already been given control.

Dangerous Steps

The trembling nervousness left me after the first beer, and I entered into the spirit around me. Everything seemed pleasant enough, although Sam was on high alert and extremely tense.

The rest of the evening is patchy to me, but my next memory is sitting down to dinner back at the Castle. I recall that the food was absolutely exquisite, and Sam was filling my glass with an expensive white wine; however, there was no joy in the moment, as Sam sat opposite me as a boiling, bubbling-over furnace of rage and fury.

Under his breath he was cursing me and calling me the foulest names I have ever heard spoken, and the character assassination was beyond anything I have ever experienced or even imagined possible. I began to cry quietly, unable to hide or control my emotion, as the hurt and shock was extreme. Our waiter noticed and asked if everything was okay for us; Sam quickly answered him that I just had a little too much to drink.

The next memory I have of that fateful night was sitting around a huge fireplace with a roaring fire, along with other castle guests and Sam, who was scowling and looking like an extremely dangerous and evil wild beast. I am not sure if the others noticed the black hate that was pouring out of him towards me in his looks and mannerisms. I couldn't miss it, but the alcohol was numbing the earlier hurt I had felt and was replacing it with a determination to end the relationship as soon as we returned home.

In looking back, I believe that he was detecting this change of heart in me, and it was fueling his pure rage and contempt for me.

I excused myself from the group to find the ladies room. I turned a corner into the main foyer, and as I heard a noise on the other side of it I turned to see Sam very quickly disappear up the steps towards our room. Wondering what he was up to, I continued my search for the restrooms.

My Worst Moment

With great relief I located my destination, and I was pushing the door open when suddenly I felt a huge impact of force in the center of my back, which propelled me skidding across the room on the very heel of my high-heeled boots, leaning backwards the whole way so that when I hit the sinks ahead of me at waist height with great force, my upper body was propelled forward with speed. My head struck and smashed the mirror above the sink, and from there the side of my face slammed into the side of the marble sink. There was such an impact from this that my whole body was flung backwards from the sheer momentum of the initial shove at the bathroom door. I landed on my back, having my breath knocked out of me and again slamming my head on the cold stone floor.

At this point I was completely dazed, and all I could focus on was the seemingly amplified sound of a dripping faucet. In my confused brain, I thought that the noise was from the blood that was filling my eyes and trickling down my face and dripping to the cold stone floor.

My reverie over this oddity was abruptly ended with a sharp searing pain and the cracking of one of my ribs. I turned my head and body to see who my attacker was, as Sam pulled back his leg for another powerful kick to the center of my chest!

The pain was excruciating and I caught sight of how cruelly pointed and hard-nosed his boots were as they flashed by my face. Fear grew suddenly inside me and I knew I was going to die without help; I realized that I was being beaten to death.

Sam was screaming foul obscenities at me and about me, all of them untrue and insane, and the screaming of each evil, foul name was followed by a powerful kick to my shattering rib cage. With each foul curse came more crushing blows to every part of my body, and I heard the gushes of air being forced out of my throat with the powerful impacts. I was scared to scream for help, as I knew that filling my lungs with air would cause them to burst when the next crushing impact came.

I heard and felt the agonizing pain of more ribs snapping, and I knew I was about to die. All along I had been telling him that I loved him, that I didn't understand, and I asked him over and over why he was doing this. I told him he was going to kill me, and that seemed to excite him, not slow him down!

I mustered all my bravery and filled my lungs with air to scream for help. Halfway through this scream, I heard the rupture of one of my lungs, and it sounded just as you would imagine an orange would sound when driven over by the wheel of a car. The pain was indescribable and I nearly lost consciousness, but he knelt and caught my upper body before I hit the floor once again and I thought he was showing me mercy. With one hand he gently took hold of my hair, and with a smile on his face he commenced to bash the back of my head on the stone floor over and over again, with all his huge strength.

I didn't die that night, because God needed me to live, to tell other women that it doesn't matter what you've been through; you can live again like I did. You can love again and enjoy the small things that always brought you joy. You can find real love and have real relationships with good, loving people who care about you. Life is not over, and it is never too late to start again.

All these blessings are possible if you will take Jesus' hand and give your life over to Him. He will take the broken pieces of you and fashion something beautiful.

Escaping Disaster

I survived, but not without severe injuries, such as a head injury, shattered rib cage, a burst lung, nerve damage up and down my right side, ripped muscles in my neck, severe bleeding in my chest cavity, and the memory of his evil, demonic, leering face of hate.

One of the night waiters had heard my call for help, and in an effort to help me, he called one of the women from the group by the fire to come help me. He was too scared to enter the room himself and face Sam.

The girl came and crouched over my body and put her hand out towards Sam's raised foot–and I will never forget her bravery! He threw a few more half-hearted kicks as he spat at me and left in a fury. I saw him leave, and he furiously made his way up the stone stairs once again to the bedroom.

I asked my new friend to help me walk, and in my desperation I demanded that she help me outside and to the forest nearby.

It was a freezing temperature level outside, and an icy sleet was falling in torrents. Our clothes were thin, and soon we were completely soaked.

When we reached the woods, she refused to go further, and just then we heard Sam shouting at us to come to him. He had pulled up with his car and was demanding that I go with him. He was fleeing the crime scene, and he wanted me as the evidence to go with him. I begged my new friend to come with me, but when she wouldn't, I parted from her and ran as well as I could into the cover of the woods. I went a little farther before lying down under fallen branches and staying very still and quiet for at least an hour, until I felt certain that he was no longer prowling the edge of the trees shouting for me, trying to trick me to give up my location.

The icy sleet that soaked me to the skin was bone-chilling, and I tried to control the chattering of my teeth, in fear that he would hear how close I lay to his feet tramping nearby, searching the blackness for me.

In my mind I cried out to God and I demanded for Him to help me. I rudely and disrespectfully screamed inwardly for Him to appear right then and help me know what to do. I told Him that if He was real, then this was the time I really needed Him to prove it to me. I didn't expect an answer, and for a few seconds I sank deeper into the darkness about me. All that I heard were my raspy breaths and the demonic man yelling angrily for me to come back to him and forsake my hiding place.

Then God's voice spoke, to my mind, in a voice rich with calm authority. The words were bold and clear and were firmly imprinted forever on the canvas of my mind.

He told me, "You will move abroad," and in my delirium I dared to question Him, "What about Ralf (my little dog)–I cannot leave him!" God told me, "He will go with you." Foolishly I responded again with, "But my house–how can I leave what I have struggled so hard to have again?" God told me, "You will rent out your house; it will be ok."

49

Even now I can't believe it, but I then said to Him, "But God, what about my mother's furniture which is precious to me?" Without ever changing His tone, God replied, "You will store your furniture, but you will have more, better furniture."

I asked more irrelevant, mindless, dumb questions, but God had told me all that I needed to know for the next steps of my life.

He was getting ready to move me out of "my Egypt" and into His plan for my life, despite the mess I had made of my life.

Struggle for Freedom

When I first cried out to God, I was really hoping for Him to rescue me from the dire situation I was in at the moment, but He did even better than that. He gave me hope for a better future, something to look towards. At the moment, however, I was left with figuring how to get out of the woods by myself. I guess that He figured I could manage that part of it, and I have no doubt that He was helping me even when I could not hear or see Him.

How I managed to scale an eight-foot metal spiked fence, with no lateral bars other than at the very top, I don't know. Only God knows the answer to that part of the story. I found a few kind souls who called the police for me and I made it to a nearby hospital, where they said my injuries were too severe for them to treat; and in addition to the injuries, I now had hypothermia as well. I was to be transferred to another location, and then I saw Sam enter the hospital on a security camera and started to scream in fear.

No one could calm me and I was seriously scared for the young policeman who was standing guard over me.

Sam had previously shared with me that he was tortured by a dream of how he had once beaten a policeman to death, and had

50

crushed the man's head with a hammer. I had dismissed this as a nightmare, but now it bounced back into my mind with credibility and I knew it was an actual guilty memory of his!

Sam reached my bedside, despite flustered nurses asking him to leave and commanding me to lie down. He demanded that I leave with him (in Ireland at that time the hospital staff or police had no authority to detain me against my will, even for my own well-being), and I don't know why I decided to leave with him, but I like to think that I had the young policeman's safety at heart or that I wanted to retrieve my beloved little dog, Ralf, from Sam's house. Whatever the truth was, I ripped an I.V. from my arm and I hobbled to his car with him, and I shook with cold and fear for three days as a hostage at his house.

I could not move, and I certainly could not drive my car which was parked at his house; and he refused to take me to a relative's house. I missed work, and because of the timing of missing shifts on New Year's Eve and New Year's Day, I also lost my job. This news reached the ears of one of my sisters, and she started to try to contact me. She realized something was very wrong and eventually discovered that I must be badly hurt and confined in Sam's house.

Unknown to me, my sister contacted the police and she was told the whole story. On her advisement, the police decided to surround the house and make preparation to forcibly remove me.

I had to deal with Sam's advances during that time, even though I was in extreme agony. During baths I had to listen to him sob uncontrollably as he knelt down beside me, while I tried to wash dried blood and mud out of my hair, with clumps of it coming out in my hands.

When I was able to, I said my goodbyes to a broken, sick Sam and left, before any police intervention was taken, and while Sam was in a mood to allow me to. After that, Sam attempted to get me back and started to stalk all members of my family. I stayed with my father for a few weeks while I began to recover and figure out my immediate future.

I never did really get an explanation from Sam for why he did what he did, and he left me with a huge bill to pay from Castle Leslie, as he had ordered approximately ten bottles of expensive wine and had destroyed the bedroom where we were to stay. He had also destroyed all my clothes and makeup. The management of Castle Leslie, however, were extremely kind to me and took upon themselves the expense of the damage that he caused to their property, and all the wine that he drank. I am extremely grateful to them for their mercy and kindness.

Police helicopters flew over my father's house at night during this time, using search lights as they conducted a search for Sam. We learned that he was very much wanted by the police on any charge they could get him for, because as it turned out, he was a very active member of an Irish terrorist group. He was known by the police as a murderer and an extremely dangerous man, although they never had enough evidence to convict him and the witnesses disappeared. I was about to disappear, too.

Starting From Scratch

As far as I could see, my life in Ireland was over; it was smashed to smithereens. I could no longer be safe living there with this extremely dangerous and mentally unbalanced man stalking me. I was worried about my family also, because I recalled that during the attack at Castle Leslie, he was screaming at me that he was going to murder all of my family.

I really believed that Sam was absolutely capable of anything, no matter how extreme or bizarre. So I believed that it would be best and safest for everyone if I removed myself from the situation entirely. During this time, I was strengthened by the memory of God's words to me in the dark woods and the promise that they held for the future.

My eldest sister really reached out to help me in this situation. She even contacted the pastor of the church I had been attending, to ask him if he knew of anywhere I could go to be safe until Sam stopped searching for me.

The problem wouldn't have existed if I had gone along with the police by putting in place a restraining order and by pressing criminal charges against Sam. However, I was just so scared of his revenge against me–but mostly against my family–because I really believed he was insane. So when my pastor presented an opportunity for me to travel to Northern England to be part of a ministry there, I jumped at the chance. This particular ministry belonged to Pastors Matt and Julie Beemer, who were friends of both my pastor and his wife.

It was nerve-wracking for me to hide my car from Sam at my father's house, gather a few clothes and essentials together in a suitcase, and say goodbye to my father and my little Ralf. I was leaving behind a life that I had built up from the ashes, to go into the unknown with virtually nothing in my possession, and to connect with people who were strangers to me.

I was going to be starting over again from scratch, but at the same time, I was tired of feeling scared.

So I made a decision to trust God, and to embrace with an open mind all that I might learn at this new church about Him and about being a Christian.

I didn't see any other better options. I had tried every other avenue that might lead to peace and happiness, and none had produced any good fruit–only bad, rotten fruit. My experiences had left me delusional, disappointed, worn down, and finally almost dead. So I really didn't have anything to lose.

Key Points Review

➤ All of God's blessings are possible if you will take Jesus' hand and give your life over to Him. He will take the broken pieces of you and fashion something beautiful.

➤ God was getting ready to move me out of "my Egypt" and into His plan for my life, despite the mess I had made of my life.

➤ I have no doubt that God was helping me even when I could not hear or see Him.

➤ During this time, I was strengthened by the memory of God's words to me in the dark woods.

➤ I made a decision to trust God, and to embrace with an open mind all that I might learn about Him and about being a Christian.

Ask Yourself...

Do I know anyone who is in an abusive situation right now? How might God want me to pray more intently for that person?
Why are we allowed to encounter pain and suffering?
What specific things has God spoken to me in the past that have stayed with me ever since?
In what areas of my life can I trust God more?

Read Romans 8:37-39. List out any painful or difficult aspects of your life in which God wants to give you greater victory, put today's date next to them, and commit them to God in prayer. When you see victory come to that area in the future, add a "victory date" next to it.

Chapter 6

INTO THE ARMS OF AMERICA

Upon arriving at Manchester airport, I was met by a most kindly lady who simply exuded love. Being with her helped me to feel more secure, although I couldn't connect entirely with her. When I was in her company, I saw myself as a dirty, foul-natured person, with secrets and darkness in my heart.

I acted in a way that was charming and pleasant, but I felt like a con artist and a counterfeit around her. I was pretending to be a good person and a happy person, and I was sure that she could see right through me and my pretensions.

I settled into a home with other Christian ladies, but I was often alone and lonely, and I let alcohol and cigarettes start to slip back into my evenings.

I secured a paid position at the church's coffee shop, and that lifted my mind and took some of the financial fear from me. On my days off, I sat at the back of the Bible School classes, and I began to learn about Jesus and His Word more than ever before. When I heard about salvation, I wanted that, and I asked right away for the pastor's wife to pray with me and walk me through the process. I so much wanted to make sure that I did it absolutely 'perfectly', because I knew this was something that I had to get right!

Shortly after that, Jesus brought to my memory the time when I was four years old, and how I had once dedicated my life to Him, thirty-three years earlier. Right away after receiving Jesus once again into my heart, I began to feel a change inside me. I felt hope again, and I felt like I had a clean slate in life and a real chance for happiness, security, and peace.

With this hope, much of my joy and sense of humor returned; and the feeling of being a filthy, flawed human was diminishing, even though I still had evenings when I would secretly drink and smoke and then hide it from my new Christian friends. I knew within myself that it would only be this way for a short season, and that soon I would be delivered from my addictions.

I knew that as I pressed in close to Jesus and read His Word,
He would remove all the impurities from within me.

An Unexpected Message

After almost three months in my new Christian environment, I began to miss my home and my wee Ralf and all things familiar. So I made arrangements to return home, and without telling anyone I bought an airline ticket to Ireland in one week's time.

Two days after I purchased my ticket, one of my mature Christian friends approached me with tears in her eyes. She went on to tell me how she had heard from God while in prayer for me. He had told her that I had made plans to leave and to encourage me to stay just a little bit longer.

At first I was skeptical that anyone could actually hear God so specifically, but He reminded me how He had once spoken very clearly to me, so I decided to trust that this lady had heard from God and to trust that He knew what was best for me. I tore up my ticket and waited with expectancy to see what God had in store for my life.

This short season of my life was the turning point in God's plans for me, turning away from darkness and walking towards the light. I chose to leave destruction, lies, and depression, and to run instead towards freedom, joy, and love!

Here is my prayer of thankfulness:

Jesus, You made Yourself so real to me during that time through the Christian people around me. They loved me while I was still unlovable, they treated me with honor while I was dishonorable, and they treated me like I was worth something when I felt worthless.

I will be eternally grateful to those great people who changed the course of my life, by showing me Your love for me, Jesus.

Jesus, thank You for forgiving me of all my sins and for washing me with Your precious blood, back unto righteousness. I received You then as my Lord and Savior, and every day now I lay my life down at Your feet. Please do with my life what You will; I give it to You.

As I have learned to do this more and more, my peace and fulfillment are much greater, and the temptations for me to fall into sin are much less powerful.

This is what the Lord says— your Redeemer, the Holy One of Israel: "I am the Lord your God, who teaches you what is best for you, who directs you in the way you should go."
(Isaiah 48:17 NIV)

From the beginning, I was taught that really pressing into God and reading His Word daily, letting it wash my mind and renew my ways of thinking, would be required if I was to see God really move in my life and restore all that had been lost.

At the beginning of my Christian walk, I still operated in a very worldly way. It took quite a lot of time for me to renew my mind, and God knew that I needed natural help in order to change completely. This came in the form of strong Christians around me, who would in love correct me and steer me off the broad-beaten path and onto God's narrow road!

Christopher Shingleton

The weekend after I tore up my ticket to fly home, the church was holding an international convention, to which various ministers were invited from around the world. The guest speaker was none other than my pastor from Northern Ireland, Paul Brady. I was delighted to see him and his wife Karen, as they represented to me a little piece of home.

One of the people invited to the ministers' convention was a Mr. Christopher Shingleton, an American pastor and personal friend of Pastors Matt and Julie Beemer, who were hosting the event. Chris had attended Rhema Bible College with Matt and Julie back in the early 1990s and had pastored in different locations and churches throughout Pennsylvania in the USA.

The friendship between Matt and Chris was over a decade old, and Matt was aware that life had taken a hard turn for Chris and that he had been struggling for some time with circumstances in his life. Chris's story is his own, but it is sufficient to mention that he had recently been through a traumatic divorce, during which he had been separated from his beloved children, and his ministry simultaneously was derailed.

Chris was bruised and beaten up by multiple betrayals, and he had reached a very low point in his life. Matt knew that the convention and a reconnection with other ministers would be good for Chris, and he encouraged him to make the trip to England. Chris, however, had simultaneously received an invitation from an old wayward friend to accompany him on a wild trip to Las Vegas!

Chris was torn between the two invitations, as he felt worn out in ministry but also felt that he deserved to blow off some steam and escape his sad reality for a weekend. Matt finalized the decision by purchasing an airline ticket for Chris, putting an end to his indecision.

When I first saw Chris walk into the coffee shop, he stood out to me as someone of interest. During the weekend I saw him occasionally, and I noted his openness and friendliness. He seemed kind, and I was cautiously interested in him.

On the second evening of meetings, I was serving in the church café when Chris suddenly appeared in front of me with his hand outstretched. "Hi," he grinned like Don Johnson, "I am Chris Shingleton; it's nice to meet you!" Immediately, I knew that this man would be my husband, if I wanted it to be so. I barely heard his next words, as a rush of thoughts raced through my brain. I thought of God's Word to me in the black woods, that I would live abroad and followed by the thought, "This must be why God wanted me to stay a little longer in England!" This was then followed by another thought, "He's good looking–nice smile!"

Despite the devil's efforts to prevent Chris and me from meeting, we did meet and quickly discovered our similarities: our shared sense of humor, our similarly painful pasts, and our equal desires to end our cycles of torment and to find lasting happiness and unity with God and each other. It was such an exciting time, with so many preparations to be made; Ralf and I were going to emigrate to America, and Chris and I were to be married and to start an amazing, exciting new life together!

Within five months of hearing God speak loudly to me that dark night, everything He said came to pass.

I moved to live abroad with Ralf, my house was rented out, and my precious furniture was stored at my Dad's house!

At the release of this book we just celebrated 10 years of marriage!

America

Emigrating to America was one of the most life-changing events to ever happen to me. It was definitely God's deliverance in my life, rescuing me from a very destructive lifestyle and environment. He brought me to a country where I was surrounded by believers who helped disciple me and encourage me in my walk with Jesus.

From his previous marriage, Chris had four beautiful children: two boys and two girls. It required a mental adjustment for me to suddenly find myself to be a step-mom to four children I had only just met, but I have to say, they made it very easy for me! I had never met such adorable, loving, and giving souls. They were a joy to be around from the beginning and have remained that way all these years.

My new life was bright and I suddenly had caring,
loving people all around me.

My old life was far behind me, and there was so much for me to learn about my new life. It was a wonderful time for me, and I was excited and expectant for what the future held for me.

However, I wasn't instantly fixed by any means, for I had to learn how Jesus would have me live, and then I had to put this new way of living into practice! I admit that it took me some time to change my thoughts, habits, and beliefs. It wasn't always easy to change, and in fact it was pretty difficult; at times, I fell very short of my own expectations of myself and of other people's expectations as well. At these times, I was extremely disappointed with myself and I felt I had let other people down – principally, my husband Chris.

One instance of a huge relapse into my old ways of living came at a time when I had started to feel secure in my new life of stability. I started to falsely believe that I was now at a place in my life where I was strong in myself and no longer vulnerable to falling back into old addictions. I believed that they could never have any power over me again.

I thought that a small liquor or an occasional glass of wine was something that normal people would drink. Now that I had a good sense of boundaries, a new-found self-control, and a proper sense of priorities, I thought that I could handle drinking alcohol like a 'normal' person.

How so very, very wrong and deceived I was to ever believe this! I had taken God out of the equation and was relying on my own strength and wisdom. Consequently, the devil made sure that my favorite liquor, Bailey's Irish cream, was made available to me in an ungodly environment devoid of any accountability whatsoever, and in my foolishness I thought I could handle one relaxing sip. Well, I couldn't handle one sip! I nearly finished the entire bottle.

It had been a long time since I had touched alcohol, and I was completely unprepared for how it affected me. It seemed that the addiction had grown in size and intensity even though I had quit drinking years before, and my re-involvement with it gave me a horrifying glimpse of how it had been smoldering and growing in its deadliness behind the scenes.

Growing Pains

My short-lived re-engagement with alcohol produced the most horrendous, heart-stopping terror and utterly devastating shame for me. It made me violently ill, which I was unable to hide from the ungodly people that I was unfortunately around at that very time.

Shock and shame grew intensely in my mind and threatened to completely steal my sanity. At that moment, I foolishly expressed the desire to just die rather than have to face the consequences of this massive failure. The inevitable shame, humiliation, guilt, and disappointment that were surely coming would be too enormous for me to handle, I thought. I could not imagine being able to survive this kind of failure at this point in my life.

The wrong ears heard me say that I would rather die, and the authorities were contacted.

The Baker Act is a mental health act that allows the involuntary institutionalization and examination of an individual who is deemed to be a danger to self or others.

As I had expressed a desire for self-harm, although it was just a foolish, self-pitying, meaningless statement for me, I nevertheless found myself under the Baker Act, initiated by law enforcement officials who had been called to the scene. The unthinkable, unimaginable scenario for me then unfolded. I was admitted to a mental institution for evaluation.

Different people throughout my life had meanly insinuated that I needed to live in a mental hospital due to my raging alcohol addiction, but I never believed that I had any actual mental conditions underneath the physical addiction. The head psychiatrist confirmed this in the institution, and I was released in record time, with a stern recommendation to seek counsel for addictions and to pursue rehabilitation.

My experience in that institution would be the worthy content of a whole other book! Up to that point in my life, I had never been faced with such unfathomable fear. I shook the entire time I was there, because the evil around me was palpable.

God spoke clearly to me during the three hideously long hours that I was locked in that prison of doom and despair. He told me to reach out and help others around me—that this was the only thing I could do that would help me to survive my terrifying time in that place. My time there was filled to the maximum capacity with sickness, insanity, and a devouring evil.

With Jesus' strength, however, I led three fellow inmates to the Lord! Thank You, Jesus, that something good came from the worst event in my life!

I now remember to always plead the blood of Jesus over such institutions, over the demon-afflicted inmates, and over the doctors and people who work there so selflessly.

I learned that I am never going to be exempt in this life from the temptations of the devil, or from his lies that would tell me that I have now reached a place where I can handle alcohol, or that in my own strength I can live successfully for any length of time.

I now admit that I am fully dependent on God - on His strength and on His wisdom!

Learning Together

Amazingly, Chris stood by me and never stopped loving me and supporting me. We were able to eventually bounce back fully restored from all that occurred during that tough, tough time. I was also blessed with the support of my pastors and loving parents-in-law. I told no one else.

Our fledgling marriage survived through some stormy waters. I had two miscarriages, and we sometimes had relational challenges also. Too often we would fall into the recurring temptation to fight for what we felt were our rights, and so we indulged in large amounts of strife at times.

We had both come recently out of damaging relationships and both had a lot of healing to do, but we have never stopped believing that God had put us together for His purpose. We knew He was aware of our hurts and weaknesses, and yet He put us together at that time in our lives when a new marriage may not have seemed the wisest choice. But he brought us together for a reason: for our own good. So we chose to trust Him to work out our lives and our marriage.

As long as we always remember to stay close to Him and continue to read His Word daily to renew our minds, all remains well with us. We have grown up in Him and have learned to love Him, ourselves, and each other with His love, unconditionally. Any moment that we relax our close walk with Jesus, our relationship cannot maintain its strength, and before we know it we find ourselves in discord within our home.

Jesus continues to be the key, and it has become more and more glaringly obvious that He is the only way that anyone will make it in their personal lives and in marriage.

It was at this point of knowledge that I gladly handed over my marriage, along with everything else, to God. With Him all things are possible, and when we respond to each other as He would have us respond, and when we keep our love for each other active, we live peaceably together and the home is a place of safety and joy. All glory and thanks to Jesus!

When our adorable daughter Tessa entered the world, the most unexplainable joy and love of life came with her! Suddenly, everything which had become old, tainted, and humdrum for me was reinvigorated back to life. Christmas reclaimed its sparkle and mystique; Chris was the ultimate Santa Claus, and the whole season takes on an excitement that I have not felt since I was very young.

Tessa was a dream baby. God really gave me a sweet child who is so easy to love, nurture, and cherish. She has brought so much joy back into my life!

Chris and I have never quit learning, forgiving, growing, and loving one another, through all that came against us. I can say now that every moment was worth it for all that I have learned, and for what is now a wonderful family of seven: Chris, me, Tessa, Victoria, Judah, Luke, and Annalise! I always wanted a large family, but could not envision having all those babies!

God works out all our needs and desires in a perfect way
when we submit our lives to Him.

Now I am happy to say that my life is healthy, happy, and productive; God took me from slavery to a place of safety and joy, where I am able to help others find their way out of bondage and into their promised land, just like me.

Never again do I want to play the role of God in my life. I can say with 100 percent sincerity that I surrender my life and my will to Him. I am dead, and He is alive in me!

Thank You, Jesus, for seeing me through such hard, terrifying, shameful times. Without You I would be in utter, utter defeat, instead of victory!

Key Points Review

➤ I knew that as I pressed in close to Jesus and read His Word, He would remove all the impurities from within me.

➤ *This is what the Lord says— your Redeemer, the Holy One of Israel: "I am the Lord your God, who teaches you what is best for you, who directs you in the way you should go."* (Isaiah 48:17 NIV)

➤ Within five months of hearing God speak loudly to me that dark night, everything He said came to pass.

➤ I now admit that I am fully dependent on God–on His strength and on His wisdom!

➤ God works out all our needs and desires in a perfect way when we submit our lives to Him.

Ask Yourself...

Do I believe that God can speak His specific messages to me through another person?
Am I willing to move out of my comfort zone if that is what God wants me to do?
Have I ever had moments of relapse into sinful habits of the past? How did I respond?
Is my marriage and/or family focused on growing together in God's principles?

Read II Peter 3:17-18. Then take a few minutes as a family or as a prayer group to discuss how you can grow in grace together.

Conclusion

Eternal Perspective

M y prayer is that others who find themselves in destructive life patterns may read my testimony and know that all things are possible with Jesus.

I teach my daughter now that to have a happy, productive life, it is necessary to walk closely with Jesus throughout life, in every occasion. She knows now that it is possible to have peace and tranquility in her heart, no matter what life throws her way, because Jesus is always with her and her hope is in Him and not in the things of this world.

We have an eternal perspective now and know that our lives are not our own but belong to Jesus, our Savior, in whose loving arms we will soon be, forever and ever. We know that Heaven is a real place, and that with Him in our hearts His power and authority are ours to wield here on earth! We know that with Him we need not fear evil and darkness, but can always expect victory. This is my hope for you!

As I was speaking recently at a women's gathering, I recounted my testimony in order to show others that no matter what we go through, there is always hope! There is hope in our Lord Jesus to release us from the snares of our enemy. There is hope to set us free and to set us apart from the lusts and desires of this world.

Jesus calls us to be in the world but not of the world. So many of us get the wrong idea that once we are set free, we need to protect and separate ourselves from the world. Because of this, we cocoon ourselves in the Church and surround ourselves with like-minded Christian people only. But how are we to affect and help change a sick and dying world if we are not in it? We must shed the light and love of Jesus on others who are still living in darkness, and we must tell our testimonies of how He set us free and replaced our pain and despair with joy and love and eternal life!

We are to be the salt and light in the earth; we are in these last days to be working as harvesters for Jesus, seeking the lost and leading them home. I want Jesus to say to me one day, "Good job and well done, you faithful servant."

Now that I know His plans and purposes for us, I so desire to be busy about the Lord's work, loving Him, receiving His great love, and pouring it out on others! What else really matters compared to this? What else has such eternal significance?

Let's remember that what is impossible for man is possible with God! (Mark 10:27)

I wonder at the hopelessness Moses could have felt when facing the Red Sea with the three million Israelites and the Egyptian army bearing down on them, or how Joshua could have despaired when staring at the walls of Jericho. Gideon's heart could have failed when he and his 300-man army faced the huge army of the Midianites, or Paul and Silas could have accepted their seemingly hopeless situation when chained and imprisoned.

But no! These men knew God, and they were obedient to His directives and trusted that what He had promised would come to pass. They overlooked their own fleshly misgivings and shortcomings and relied on God, and God kept His promises! Moses saw God part the Red Sea; Joshua saw the walls of Jericho crumble and fall; Gideon defeated the Midianite army with ease, and the chains fell off Paul and Silas as their prison burst open!

In the same way, God promises to be your Savior, to be your Rock, to keep your foot from stumbling, to set you free, and to lift you to dry ground! Believe Him today for whatever you need, and never quit believing in the Anchor of your soul! Our Lord Jesus has promised to be faithful, and He will see you through.

I can do all things through Christ who strengthens me.
(Philippians 4:13)

Putting God First

Shortly after the beginning of my ministry of restoration, God showed me that I was just like the Israelites that He rescued from Egypt. I also was rescued from bondage and captivity, just as they were.

After they were rescued, the Israelite people fell into sin by worshipping foreign gods and idols. Unbelievably, I too was found lacking in my devotion to God, even after He had done so much for me.

He had literally taken me out of a life of severe tormenting emotions of guilt, shame, depression, and fear. He had brought me to a new land. Instead of a life of addiction, He had given me real love with a wonderful, beautiful, joyful life; instead of fear, He had given me peace; instead of guilt and shame, He had given me joy; and instead of Hell, He had given me eternal life.

And yet in this wonderful new life something was still missing. God's full blessings were somehow being withheld from me and my family, and we struggled financially even when we believed we were living righteously and when we tithed and loved God.

God began to reveal to me that I was not fully putting Him first in my life, and that there were things that I clung to more tightly and that I cared for more than Him. I had brought over money with me from Ireland, and we had invested in a beautiful home here in America, and there was enough left over to garnish it with furniture to my exact taste.

I guarded fiercely the money in this new home and the furniture within it. I was very protective over my beautiful home image, and I was unwilling to take some of this money from selling one gorgeous home for another and to do some traveling ministry with it. God had promised that He would replenish the money like the loaves and fishes in the Bible, but I did not fully trust Him.

I missed this opportunity to do His will and to help others with our message, and God revealed to me that the house, money, and possessions that I was putting before Him were in fact idols to me! When I realized the truth of this, I was undone with sadness and fell on my knees in repentance. I had been in sin, worshipping idols without even being aware of it.

When we are in sin, we close doors and shut off God's blessings to us, but we do open other doors to the enemy, to bring lack and hardship along with our sin.

As soon as I truly saw my covetous nature and the error of it and repented for it, the floodgates of financial blessings opened and flowed over us! It was amazing and God poured His supernatural blessings upon us, once I had learned to find my identity in Him and not in the things of this world. I realized that all that we have is His and not ours, and we need to depend on Him for all things.

Through this season of growth in my Christian walk, I saw so clearly how God loved me! I saw how much He loved the Israelites—to save them from Egypt, to part the Red Sea, and to keep on loving them even after they fell into sin. That's how much He loves me, and you, if you also are a part of His family.

Now I check my heart every day to make sure that no covetous seeds are growing there, and that my identity is firmly planted in Him, my Lord and Savior Jesus Christ.

About the Author

Freida currently resides in the United States with her husband Christopher and their daughter Tessa, plus a small envoy of fluffy pets!

She works faithfully at Campus Crusade for Christ with The Jesus Film Project and is keen to see the world reached for Jesus.

An avid speaker, she loves to share her testimony of the restoration and grace she has found in Christ and to bring hope to those that are lost and trying to find escape from the devil's bondages.

Prayer for Salvation

Please pray the following and be instantly grafted into the family of God. Receive His love, forgiveness, joy and all the blessings that He has provided for you here on earth and for all eternity! There is nothing to lose and everything to gain!

Dear God, I come to You just as I am in the name of Jesus. I acknowledge to You that I am a sinner, and I am sorry for my sins and the life that I have lived without You; I need Your forgiveness.

I believe that Your only Son, Jesus Christ, shed His precious blood on the cross long ago, and died for my sins, and I am now willing to turn from my sin and my own ways.

At this very moment I confess Jesus as the Lord of my life. With my heart, I believe that God has raised Jesus from the dead. Right now I accept Jesus Christ as my own personal Savior and according to Your Word, right now I am saved.

Thank You, Jesus, for Your unlimited grace which has saved me from my sins. I thank You, Jesus, for this new life and endeavor to serve You from this time forward.

I am so grateful that You have given me eternal life. AMEN

Suggested Additional Reading

A Time to Heal – Beyond Survival
Sue Willis

Out of Islam – One Muslim's Journey to Faith in Christ
Christopher Alam

The Believer's Authority
Kenneth E. Hagin

Conquering Demons – To Be Free. To Set Free.
Christian Hedegaard

CPSIA information can be obtained
at www.ICGtesting.com
Printed in the USA
LVOW13s0848230517

535454LV00006BA/17/P